Graduate School on a Budget

*Define Your Life By What You Learn,
Not By What You Owe*

LAURA H. GILBERT, PH.D.

For the next generation of graduate students.

May you graduate
with a job in hand and money to spare.

Acknowledgments

Special thanks to my dear friend and editor, Beverly Pierce. Her careful eye and librarian's logic added precision and clarity to each chapter. This book is much stronger because of her contributions. Thank you Bev!

And a special thank you to the nine current and former graduate students who contributed their insightful and entertaining stories to this book. Each writer approached education with a dual goal: earn a highly regarded graduate degree as cost-effectively as possible. Their practical wisdom proves it is possible to earn a graduate degree on a budget. Thank you and congratulations!

Table of Contents

Chapter Two: Academic Expenses 15

Chapter Three: Life Expenses. 29

Chapter Four: Managing Debt 41

Introduction

Congratulations! As a recent college graduate you now hold the primary prerequisite for graduate school admission: a bachelor's degree. Your undergraduate degree opens the door for you to apply to pursue a master's, doctoral, law or medical degree. But should you? And how can you do so without going broke? If these are your questions, this book was written for you!

Why Attend Graduate School?

There are many good reasons to further one's education but also reason to be cautious. Some suggest a master's degree or an MBA is the new bachelor's degree; in other words, an unspoken prerequisite for a good job. Others view a law degree as the new MBA. Why? Those with less-common, rigorous, advanced education may stand out in a stack of resumes.

Past trends suggest lifetime earnings increase as one earns academic degrees (BA, MA, MBA, JD, PhD, MD). Yet that data is based on an old model of how the world and workplace work. Although the data is still in your favor, a generic advanced degree no longer guarantees better job prospects and higher income. Next time you are in Starbucks, ask the baristas how many hold advanced degrees. You may be surprised.

Graduate school is also not a prerequisite for a good life. An advanced degree does not automatically make you a better person, nor does it increase the value of your personal contributions to society. The world is full of individuals making remarkable contributions without impressive credentials.

"So if I have no guarantee of more money and I'm the same good person either way, why should I bother with graduate school?" Here are three good reasons:

1. Your career goals require an advanced degree.

2. You truly believe your job prospects will increase significantly with an advanced degree AND the stress associated with earning the degree is less than the stress of always wondering what might have been.

3. It is only in graduate school that your area of interest can be studied at the level you wish.

If you've decided graduate school is the path for you, the next tasks are (1) to find the program that best fits your long-term goals, and (2) to fund this venture through means that allow you to:

Define your life by what you learn, Not by what you owe.

Although a few students earn full rides or small scholarships, most fund graduate school through cash and loans — lots of loans. The sheer cost of graduate school can lead to "Monopoly brain", where spending $20, $200 or even $2000 feels about the same. In a couple short years, the graduate student can find herself holding a lovely diploma in one hand and $75,000 or more of debt documents in the other. In *Graduate School on a Budget*, you'll learn tricks and tips to get the education you want for a price that allows you to sleep at night.

Who should read this book? [1]

Are you:

+ A college junior or senior?
+ A student who has been out of college for five years or less?
+ Twenty-something?

Do at least <u>three</u> of these describe you?

+ Started college within two years of high school graduation.
+ Still searching for a career path.
+ Need a graduate degree for your chosen career path.
+ Have begun but not settled deeply into a first career.
+ May own a car but not a house.
+ May be in a serious relationship but are not married.
+ May have a pet or plants but not children.
+ May have debts but not DEBTS.

---

1 *Graduate School on a Budget* is the second in a set of three books on cost-saving tips for students. The first book, "How to Save $50,000 on College", teaches 16-24 year olds how to make the most of their education dollar. The third, "Curbing College Costs as an Adult Learner", tackles the special needs of adult students.

If so, *Graduate School on a Budget* was written for you! If, on the other hand, you are married with two kids and a mortgage, hold a full-time job, or are over thirty, skim this book then dive into the next book in this set, *Curbing College Costs as an Adult Learner.*

Why Budget?

As a recent college graduate, you know about the high cost of education. Graduate school can easily double (or triple) your current education bill. Even hefty scholarships and grants do not guarantee a debt-free education — far from it. Full-scholarship students who fail to plan for non-tuition expenses may graduate with heavy student loan debt, while financially savvy, full-pay classmates graduate with little to none.

The difference depends on you — your career goals, yes, but more importantly, your decisions along the way. I'm here to show you how.

Budget in this book means:

+ Pause before you purchase
+ Create a spending framework for expenses
+ Make intentional choices with this framework in mind

Budget in this book does not mean:

+ Skimp and starve
+ Track every penny (unless that's rewarding for you)
+ Miss out on valuable opportunities uniquely available to students

Five Reasons for a Graduate School Budget

1. Because you are about to spend a pile of money; possibly enough for a nice house.

2. Because student loan debt can creep up on you. Few students set out to borrow $100,000 or more (roughly $1000/month in payments that may cost you $200,000 or more in cash by the time it is paid off). A budget is a map to keep you on track and guide you through intentional or unplanned detours.

3. Because it is easy to overspend on non-essentials when others are doing so and you feel you deserve it too. When you reward yourself by spending loan money on non-essentials during grad school, you have to pay it all back — with interest.

4. Because five years from now it will be more fun to spend your hard-earned dollars on a house or vacation than on student loan debt.

5. And if everything comes crashing down ten years from now, you can declare bankruptcy for your bills, give back your house, car and TV, but your student loan debt lives on forever — kind of like cockroaches.

Isn't Budgeting the Same for Grads and Undergrads?

Not for most students. Remember your first semester freshman year? Everything was new: college-level coursework, personal independence, dorm living, food sources, recreation, laundry, relationships, and money management. That is a lot to learn all at once, no matter how high your SATs were! Undergraduates are like baby birds learning to fly. Some will soar. Others will crash — especially those who haven't learned to manage credit cards. Most will falter along the way but ultimately succeed.

During your undergraduate days you gained a wealth of life experience. As you approach grad school you are more financially savvy than you were at 18, simply because you've:

- Grown personally as well as intellectually
- Learned what you need in order to do well academically
- Gained clarity about the potential pay-off of an advanced degree (and reasonable loan debt) because you are:
  - Homing in on a specific career
  - Have a better idea of job prospects
  - Have a better idea of salary prospects
- Spent four years living on a limited income and making tough financial choices (or poor choices that became lessons in what not to do)

Likewise, students 26 or older with job and family responsibilities, bring extra financial burdens with them to graduate school. A 24-year-old law student can save money living with parents or in a graduate student dorm. The 40-year-old single parent of three is less likely to have the same opportunity.

Chapter Summaries

Graduate School on a Budget is organized into seven chapters. Although ordered in a plausible sequence, each chapter can stand alone. Skip around to find the information you need when you need it.

Chapter One, *Graduate School as an Investment*, shows you how to invest wisely in a graduate education starting with critical questions such as, "What do I want from graduate school?" "What are my expectations about how the degree will pay off?" "How do I know a program is worth the investment?"

Chapter Two, *Academic Expenses*, looks at cost-containment strategies for school-related expenses from tuition to technology to professional equipment and clothes.

Chapter Three, *Life Expenses*, explores cost-containment strategies for expenses you'll incur whether or not you go to grad school. Housing option pros and cons, healthcare, even entertainment as a young adult are addressed. A final section touches on how to keep on track when a major event occurs, such as a wedding, a baby or even a home purchase.

Chapter Four, *Managing Debt*, helps you identify a "reasonable" budget and debt load for your situation. Readers will learn the warning signs for the most common student loan mistakes, and how to get back on track when debt starts to pile up. Plus, a quick review of loan types and standard repayment options provides critical information for making informed choices.

Chapter Five, *Getting Hired,* shows you how to maximize your chance of getting the job you want right out of school. Though nothing is certain, the sooner you can launch your career for pay, the sooner you'll see positive cash flow into your bank account.

In Chapter Six, *How I Minimized Student Debt,* cost-conscious students share their best tips for managing graduate school expenses. These delightful and practical true stories come from current students and graduates; those with full scholarships and those with none; students from public, private and international programs; teachers, physicists, social justice advocates, artists and more.

Finally, no book on educational financing would be complete without a resource section. Chapter Seven, *Resources,* include a variety of the best Internet resources for managing graduate school debt, including budget-building sites and a debt-management calculator tied to national salary data.

Best wishes to you and happy studying!

A carefully selected graduate degree
can launch a great career.
Take the time to choose (and spend) wisely.

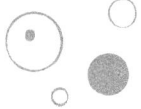

CHAPTER ONE

Graduate School as an Investment

Education is an investment — in you, in your career, and eventually in the community where you will work and live. Wise investors ask challenging questions before committing funds. What do I want from the investment? What are my assumptions about how long before the investment will pay off? How do I know the investment is trustworthy?

Whether you are investing in graduate school or the stock market, this chapter describes five truths to help you make a wise decision.

Define Your Goal — Clarify Your Costs

The two defining elements of the first analysis you'll do are:

A. Your **goal** for the an advanced degree, and

B. Your **cost** to earn the degree, measured in

- ✦ Money
- ✦ Time
- ✦ Effort
- ✦ Effect on others

A "good" investment occurs when A ≥ B; that is, when the outcome of the goal *is greater than or equal to* the total cost.

Goal clarification

The more specific your goal, the more likely you'll reach it. If your goal is simply to earn a graduate degree, you may end up with little more than a very expensive certificate for your wall. Graduate students who take a wait-and-see attitude are surprised when no one is knocking down their door with loads of cash after graduation.

Is your goal to work in a specific field, enjoy a certain lifestyle, or continue on for further education? Name it and claim it. Write it on your arm. Make it your screensaver. Search for a related ringtone. Buy the t-shirt. Do whatever you can to keep this goal in front of you from day one.

Ask yourself these questions:

- *What do you want*[2] *this graduate degree to give back to you?* Launch a specific career? Make you more marketable? Support a lifestyle? Make sure your expectations are accurate. Talk to people in the field, not just the school's marketing or admissions staff.

- *Know your audience.* Unless your goal is purely enrichment think like a sales manager — with newly credentialed you as the product. Your future employer is the buyer and all the resumes in the pile are your competitors. Who is your buyer? To whom do you want to "sell" your credentials? At which schools or programs do they primarily "shop"? Or not? Ask around. Test your assumptions.

Cost clarification

- Tuition and fees should be readily available on a school's website. For example, Concordia University (www.csp.edu) posts links to the tuition and fees for each major program on their website landing page. If a school is hesitant to share program cost, look at other schools.

- What other costs will you incur to attend the program? Is an unpaid internship required? Later chapters explore expenses beyond tuition and fees.

---

2 *Want* suggests hope whereas *expect* implies certainty. Both can be hidden assumptions best identified up front.

- What is the cost in terms of time? How long is the program? How flexible? Is there an option that allows you to work?

- What is the cost in effort? Are you a quick study or a slow reader? Do you obsess to earn top grades? Is this an intense, rigorous program that is all-consuming?

- What is the cost on friends and family? Are you single and carefree or do family and friends count on your availability and energy? Are you ready to pay the emotional price when you choose study-ing over attending a birthday celebration?

Courses and coaches are available if you want more guid-ance or support. But beware of analysis paralysis! Every higher ed cost/benefit determination yields an imprecise calculation at best. Gather enough data to feel confident in your analysis, ask a trusted advisor if you are missing (or have misinterpreted) anything major, then ask your-self, "Is the cost of graduate school worth the *potential* benefit?" Did you notice the italicized term? That brings us to the next important fact about any investment: no guarantees.

What do you want this investment
to give back to you?

Manage Your Expectations

By definition, an investment is an expenditure made today with the expectation of a favorable return in the future. Investors use past experience and research to make an educated guess that an action taken today will yield a positive result tomorrow. Nothing is guaranteed.

The same is true with grad school. The odds are in your favor it will pay off, but as a wise investor it is smart to manage a few expectations.

Manage lifestyle expectations during school (more in Chapter Three)

+ Avoid living as though you already hold a job in your field of study. Look good at networking events, but don't spend big bucks on clothes you may have to replace in two years. Save the fancy restaurants for when paychecks start coming in.

+ Remember to live like a student while you are a student, and you won't have to later.

Manage salary expectations for your first job

+ The rule of thumb for loans is to borrow no more than the low end of first-year salaries in your geographic area and industry. If you estimate too low, you'll have extra funds from each paycheck to launch a life as well as a career. If you estimate too high, you may wake up in your childhood bedroom, hoping your parents don't charge rent so you can pay your student loans.

Manage your expectations for how long it will take to land your first job

+ Perhaps you'll graduate at a time when employers are lining up to grab every possible new graduate. But, don't count on it. Save a few bucks — or goodwill from parents and friends — to help with room and board while you search.

+ Assume it may take 6 months to land your first "real" job. If you are hired the week after graduation or even earlier, celebrate. In the meantime, locate flexible, short-term employment that pays enough to live indoors while you search.

Manage your expectations for the type of first job you may find

+ Big-buck, fast-track jobs with promotional opportunities are few and far between. Budget for the likelihood you'll start at the bottom.

+ If the job market sucks, don't hold out for an A job if a B or even C+ job comes along. In a bad market it is better get *some* good experience than to tell HR you've been waiting for the right salary. If the job market is good, you won't be reading this section.

Study with high expectations.
Budget with low expectations.

Know Where You Are Investing

A graduate degree from Harvard, Stanford or another alma mater of sassy prime-time TV characters is probably a safe investment. Now, imagine this scenario:

> ABC Limited posts a job opening for a new MBA graduate. Human resources receives 500 applications. Assume 250 applicants meet the new-grad qualification. Poor presentation, typos and other factors narrow the field to 50. HR must choose 15 for phone interviews. If everything else is equal, how will HR choose? Based on my experience, this is where alma mater may figure in.
>
> ABC may reject Harvard grads, assuming they have high salary expectations or may not fit with ABC's culture. On the other hand, ABC may target the Harvard grads under the assumption they will bring expertise and drive to solve company issues. Likewise, ABC may reject grads from online programs, assuming online students didn't have the face-to-face training ABC believes is essential to be a success manager. Finally,, if a candidate who made the final 50 graduated from the alma mater of a prospective boss, a former star employee or a well-loved executive, the candidate's chance of making the top 15 improves.

Why? Because there isn't time for the hiring manager to interview each of the 500 candidates. Hiring managers must rely on their experience and knowledge base. Every school distinguishes itself through its admissions process, teaching style, academic expectations, hands-on opportunities and the student body it selects. Managers develop expectations and beliefs about graduates of

certain schools based on the performance and person-
alities of former employees from that school. Given two
otherwise-equal candidates, the manager is likely to
select the individual from the educational program he or
she knows and trusts, rather than the individual from a
lesser-known school.

If your goal is tied to working in a certain industry or
company, make sure you invest in a recognized program.
Ask career services if the industry or company recruits
from your school. This is particularly true for law or
MBA students. The best jobs typically go to top candidates from top schools. Thus, $50,000 in student loans
for a highly ranked school may be a better deal than a
full scholarship to an unknown program, if you hope to
climb a Fortune 500 ladder. Know where you, and your
program of choice, stand.

With whom will you invest?

Do Due Diligence

Once a specific investment target is identified (e.g., attending Harvard Medical School, or buying stock in Best Buy) the wise investor conducts due diligence before making the purchase. Some call this "vetting" the plan; carefully examining something to make sure it is a suitable investment before making a final decision. Business investors glean information on corporate health from annual reports, legal filings, financial audits and other standard industry records. During this exploratory phase, the wise investor checks assumptions about the strength of the investment, analyzes current data about the near-term health of the investment, and looks for weaknesses that may affect the long-term payoff.

Similarly, a wise student will conduct due diligence about prospective graduate programs; in particular, reputable career outlook data from sources outside the school. Schools may offer good information, but never forget: Their primary motivation is to convince the best applicants to sign up. The school has no obligation to place you, or help in any way. If you want to work in a specific industry or for a specific company, talk to employees. Find out what graduate programs these companies hire from — or don't hire from. It is a real shame when I see a student spend time and money on a graduate program, only to discover too late that their credential won't open the doors they thought it would.

Occasionally a single piece of data is uncovered during due diligence that becomes a deal breaker. More often, large patterns emerge that point toward a healthy decision. To make a sound investment, include research, data and opinions from multiple sources.

Due diligence resources include:

- Recent graduates from the program you are considering
  - Ask the admissions officer for names of students willing to share their experience, *but also* locate graduates on your own who aren't volunteering for the school. Ask each one:
    - What was your original goal in entering the program?
    - Do you believe your investment is paying off? Why or why not?
    - Did attendance at this program matter, or would a less expensive option have had a similar payoff?
    - What was your best investment during school (e.g., study abroad, loans to take unpaid internships)? What would you skip?
  - Note when your informant graduated. Someone who has been out 3-10 years may offer a different perspective than someone near retirement. Each is valuable.
- Hiring managers in your target industry
  - Locate hiring managers through friends, parents and social media.
  - Ask what schools they tend to hire from and why.

- + Or, ask what education-related qualities they look for, such as specific coursework, internships, or publications.

+ School websites

  + Scan the school's website for any mention of corporate partnerships.

+ Company websites

  + Scan company websites to determine if partners or senior management attended this program? If so, email or call that individual to request a few minutes to get their take on the program.

  + Scan for press releases that mention academic affiliation such as research, internships or part-time projects? If so, contact HR and ask who to speak to about these affiliations. Mention you are choosing a grad school and are particularly interested in this affiliation. Ask how graduates are selected to participate. While you have HR on this call, ask what they look for when hiring new graduates. Send a thank you note.

Think like an executive.
Take time to thoroughly vet graduate programs before you commit.

Measure Value Long-Term; Budget Near-Term

When you purchase a pair of jeans, it doesn't take long to decide if they were worth the price. If not you can take them back. Investments are different. It may take years before you can decide if an investment in higher education was worth the price. And, you can't take it back — or give it to someone else to use.

As you consider how much debt to incur in graduate school, ask yourself this: What are my assumptions about how fast the degree will (or must) pay off? How accurate is this data? Does the data reflect isolated incidents or general reality?

Many grad students expect a greatly improved salary upon graduation. It might happen. But practically speaking, a handful of students land the high-paying jobs everyone talks about. Everyone else starts at the bottom and moves up from there. Likewise, marketing brochures for graduate programs highlight stories implying that "you too" can be rich and famous. Unfortunately, marketing stories rarely describe *how long* it took for the amazingly successful alums to attain their professional achievements. Borrow only as much as you can comfortably pay off as your career builds.

In the meantime, avoid these common mistakes:

- *Don't judge the value of your investment by the salary (or prestige) of your first position.* According to a 2010 Forbes study[3], even graduates from top-

3 http://www.forbes.com/lists/2011/95/best-business-schools-11_rank.html The 2010 report includes fun facts such as "years to payback" (tuition), "pre-MBA salary," "2010 salary," "tuition" and "median GMAT score" at top-ranked schools.

ranked business schools who land big-buck jobs need about five years to get a return on their financial investment.

· *Don't borrow blindly with the assumption your first job will cover any sized loan payments.* It won't. Graduates who borrow big may find themselves holding out for a high-paying job to cover student loan payments. While they wait, low-debt peers gain job experience in a public service position or a stint with the Peace Corps.

· *Don't expect an instant shift in lifestyle upon graduation.* Be prepared to leave the student lifestyle gradually. Be patient with your ability to purchase things: new wardrobe, car, house. And by all means DO NOT take out extra student loan money in your final semester for a big vacation or other graduation splurge. Celebrate within your means. Remember, you just spent a lot of money on your future. Don't burden that future with more student loan debt. Instead, earmark that first bonus check for something really special.

Borrow based on low-end estimates of starting wages.
But, measure educational value over a lifetime.

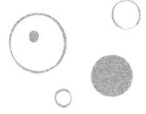

CHAPTER TWO

Academic Expenses

Although the single largest expense for an advanced degree is tuition, several other academic-related costs can tack on thousands of dollars in student loan debt. This chapter takes a close look at how to save and spend wisely on fees, books, professional equipment and clothing, as well as outside learning experiences such as study abroad programs, internships, practicums and student clinics.

Tuition

Graduate school tuition reduction options differ somewhat from undergraduate aid. Opportunities vary widely from school to school and across disciplines. Science and math grad students may have an easier time finding a fellowship or teaching assistant position than, say, students in law, medicine or the humanities. Yet persistent students in each discipline uncover opportunities to reduce the cost of tuition in spite of challenges.

The challenge: The average graduate student is likely to find that:

+ Institutional scholarships in the form of tuition discounts are less scarce.

+ Awards may cover a percentage of tuition and be renewable each term if the recipient maintains a specified grade point average each term or year. However, fall below the required GPA and the student permanently loses eligibility for the award.

+ Unlike undergrad programs, very few programs accept graduate transfer credits from other institutions, especially at the master's level. Confirm transferability of credits before taking courses outside of your program — including other programs within the institution.

+ Most philanthropic organizations that support higher education through target scholarships for undergraduate programs. The best bet to locate graduate school scholarships is to speak with a

dean, your department head, financial aid officer
and other students.

The opportunity: Graduate students may have opportunities not available to undergrads:

+ Ask about *assistantships (research and teaching), fellowships, grants and scholarships* during your initial program search. Speak with the dean or department chair <u>each term</u>. Department-specific funds change frequently.

+ If you plan to attend the school where you earned your undergraduate degree, ask about *alumni discounts* for their graduate programs.

+ If you are working, ask if your company offers *tuition reimbursement* for graduate school.

+ Seek a job at the school you wish to attend offers *tuition reduction or remission* to employees, seek a job there before you apply.

· *Study abroad.* Read Kate A.'s story in Chapter Six.

Tackle tuition from multiple angles.

Fees

Fees are separate charges added to your tuition bill each term for a variety of services and functions. Individual fees may be small, but together can add hundreds or even thousands of dollars to your bill. For instance, one middle-of-the-road three-year program charges almost $2,500 per year in fees; $7,500 over the three years. If those fees are paid with student loan funds, the total expense is likely to be 40% higher to account for interest over the life of the loan.

Standard school practice is to use an opt-out strategy regarding fees. Students are charged all fees unless they opt out before paying the bill. Yet, many fees may be options, such as a fee for student publications. Budget-conscious graduate students take time to confirm which fees are mandatory, which services they support or want, and then opt out of the rest.

Examples of fees are:

- *Student service fees* – This broad category may fund support services such as on-campus health services, student union, sports facilities, cultural and religious centers, child care centers, university-sponsored student organizations, and international service organizations related to degree programs (e.g. Engineers Without Borders). Generally mandatory.

- *College fee* – An administrative overhead fee associated with a specific program or number of credits. Mandatory.

- *Lab/supply fees* – These are associated with specific degree programs or a course. Ask if the fee includes supplies you can borrow, rent, or purchase elsewhere for less.

- *Health insurance* – Purchas health insurance, even if coverage is not mandatory. Compare the institution's plan with independent, high-deductible plans as well as the option to remain on a parent's plan (allowable up to age 26).

- *Student-directed advocacy group fees* – The national student-centered Public Interest Research Group is one example. Generally optional.

- *Student organization/club fees* – You may see a small fee on your bill for a general fund for student organizations, but student-sponsored clubs typically determine separate membership fees. Optional unless required by your program (e.g., the student chapter of a professional organization).

- *Student publications* – This fee supports student or department journalism (e.g., news, academic journals). Generally optional.

---

*Choose which optional fees
support services you want.*

Books

Thrifty graduate students understand that "required texts" means required-to-read, not required-to-purchase. Used books, shared books, e-books or books borrowed from a library or former student are excellent alternatives to paying the high cost of new books.

That said, book expenses are a good example of spending where it matters to you. Some graduate students purchase every text. Others purchase very few. Identify the alternatives and choose what works for you.

To save on books and ensure you have the resources you need:

- *Honor your learning style and academic needs.* Choose used books with care if someone else's highlighting distracts you from the content.

- *Consider the relationship between a text and class assignments.* If assignments require constant referral to a text, sharing or time-limited borrowing may not work well.

- *Do the math.* A school bookstore purchase may be more economical than an online purchase with shipping fees (or extra fees for fast delivery).

- *Build your professional library.* Certain texts that do not go out of date quickly may be useful to you throughout your career. Purchase those.

Avoid common mistakes:

- *Don't trust a previous owner's highlights or margin notes.* Never assume the previous owner earned an A. Do your own work.

- *Don't wait too long* to order books online.

- *Don't agree to share a book with the wrong person.* Different learning styles or potential availability issues may lead to disaster.

- *Don't assume* the library will have your book when you need it. If you borrow texts, have a back-up plan.

- *Waiting too long to sell them.* Editions change often. Wait, and your text may no longer be used. If you plan to sell books for cash, advertise them as soon as your course is done.

Choose which books you'll purchase.

Professional Equipment and Clothing

Graduate school prepares you to work in a specific field. While undergraduate survey courses take a broad-brush approach to large subjects (e.g., European history or statistics), graduate courses are in-depth and frequently hands-on.

Consequently, you may be required (or want) to purchase materials, equipment or clothing used by professionals in your field of study. Examples include:

- Advanced or specialized software
- Technical or scientific equipment
- Medical equipment
- Art supplies & carrying case
- Archeological tools
- Professional-quality musical instrument
- Scrubs, protective laboratory clothing
- Business suit and shoes
- Laptop with certain specifications

Take advantage of student discounts on expensive items you will use as a profession. Look for deals on items you need for one course and are rarely used outside the classroom.

Look on Craig's List. Learn who the leading suppliers are for your industry. In the process you will get to know who the key vendors are for your professions.

Ask the school how much to budget for these expenses. Then ask current students what they really spend and where they shop. The word-on-the-street is often the best source for quality deals.

Ask where current students shop.

Studying Abroad

Young professionals can safely assume their careers will reach around the globe — physically, virtually or both. Graduate-level study abroad programs are available in most disciplines, as schools strive to position their graduates for leadership roles in a global workplace.

Study abroad programs range in length from intensive week-long seminars to full-year exchanges. English is the international language of business, medicine, engineering and many other disciplines. Consequently, most study abroad programs are taught in English. However, students who want a full-immersion experience can select a program where coursework is taught in the host country's native language.

Costs and quality vary. Some charge top dollar for superb accommodations and faculty. Others place students in dreadful housing conditions with mediocre instruction for slightly less money. But note: With a little work, it may be possible to locate an exceptional study abroad program that is LESS EXPENSIVE than earning the same number of credits at your home school — including travel, room and board. Several classmates and I did it; in different programs. And the coursework and faculty were some of the best in our entire graduate experience.

To choose an excellent and economical study abroad program:

+   Look beyond programs offered by your school. Descriptions of accredited study abroad programs are published annually for many disciplines such as business, health care and law. Ask for suggestions from other students, school administrators, independent organizations that sponsor study abroad programs, and professional associations that encourage student members to gain international experience.

- Explore scholarship and grant programs that sponsor graduate-level international study (e.g., Rotary Club)

- Confirm in writing with your home school registrar that credits will transfer

- Confirm in writing whether grades from a particular study abroad program will transfer directly to your transcript or whether they will appear as "pass/fail".

- Confirm whether study abroad grades will affect your overall grade point average

- Read Kate A's story in "How I Minimized Student Debt"

- Have a blast!

Study outside the borders.

Internships, Practicums, Student Clinics, and Other Hands-On Learning Opportunities

A top-notch hands-on learning opportunity can pay off for an entire career. No course can match the experience gained or the potential to make professional connections that a real-world experience can provide.

Ask about school-sponsored opportunities (e.g., low-cost community clinics, teaching or research assistantships) as well as connections the school has to corporate-sponsored programs (e.g., internships, clerkships). Graduate school job boards may also include part-time entry-level positions for current students. Students must locate and apply for these programs, and there are no guarantees. But, in the process you'll gain invaluable insight about finding a job in the profession.

Still, choose carefully. Quality varies. Make sure you spend your time wisely. How will you describe this experience on your resume? Before accepting a position:

1. *Clarify the work* you will be doing, and with whom. Is the organization or sponsor a leader in the field? Be cautious about opportunities that claim to provide you with a mentor and a chance to do real work in your field, yet offer no specifics. Get the details ahead of time.

2. *Don't limit yourself* to considering only long-term, paid opportunities. First look for the long-term benefit, and then look at time and money. Competition for the best opportunities can be fierce, even though the work may be less interesting than one might expect. Still, a low-paid or

unpaid gig may let you showcase your talents in front of the right people and help launch your career. Or not. The point is to think long-term as you decide which, if any, hands-on opportunity to pursue.

3. *Credit-based, school-sponsored opportunities* are another option. Expect to pay tuition for the credit (a moot point if tuition is charged by the semester rather than by the credit). If you want a hands-on opportunity but need the credits, this may be a good option.

Once you start, remember you are a student auditioning as a professional.

Dress appropriately, but don't spend student loan funds on a whole new wardrobe. Play the role -but within your means. No one expects a student to look like a vice president. Outspend the budget of your immediate boss and you may even lose points for arrogance.

Buy two conservative professional outfits, whatever that means for your profession. Choose pieces that easily mix and match with basic shirts, pants or simple accessories. Cleanliness, timeliness, effort and attitude go far beyond expensive fashion to impress a potential employer.

Nothing beats a top-notch, real-world experience.

CHAPTER THREE

Life Expenses

Chapter Three looks at expenses you'll incur whether or not you are in graduate school: housing, food, transportation and health care. Yet, as a graduate student your choices may be limited by locale, school policy or personal convenience. Either way, there is money to save in each area.

A final section, *Life Moves On*, recognizes you are both a grad student and a young adult. Weddings, babies and other major events in the life of a young adult are cause for celebration; and they can quickly derail a graduate school budget without careful planning. This section shows you how.

Housing

Graduate students have a plethora of housing options, each with pros and cons.

What did your undergraduate experience teach you about your housing preferences? What do you minimally need in a living space? What three things create the best living situation for you? What is unworkable?

Where do you prefer to study? How much privacy do you need? International students often save funds by minimizing living space — really minimizing. Many live several students to a small apartment, share a car, and study at a library, coffee shop or 24-hour venue.

Know what works for you and embrace it.

Sketch out your basic needs and the top things to avoid. Then consider these options:

- **Graduate student dorm**

    Pros – On or near campus. Live with fellow students. Contract is with school rather than outside landlord. Contract may be all-inclusive (e.g., heat, electricity, internet, garbage).

    Cons – May be pricey and offer limited facilities (e.g., cooking).

- **Apartment by yourself**

    Pros – You control your immediate living environment.

Cons – You pay full cost. May have noisy non-student neighbors who don't care if you need to study. Contract may not match school year. Know what is included in rent.

+ **Apartment with roommates**

    Pros — Reduces total cost. May be able to share transportation, food, books.

    Cons — May disagree about shared expenses. If one roommate moves (voluntarily or involuntarily), you are still liable for the rent.

+ **Live with parent(s)**

    Pros – Low cost (to you, anyway). Known environment.

    Cons – Socially awkward (less so these days).

+ **Rent a room in a private home**

    Pros – Low cost. May be able to exchange room and board for babysitting, shopping for an elderly homeowner, or assisting with other household tasks.

    Cons – Be clear on expectations and the agreement with the home owner.

Consider the possibilities for long-term saving through short-term inconvenience.

Food

Graduate school may be the first time you cook your own meal on a regular basis, unless you live at home or take a full meal plan at the school cafeteria. As you set up your kitchen keep your student budget in mind. There will be plenty of time to establish a fine kitchen when your salary permits. In the meantime, here are some starter tips to save on meals and meal prep.

- *Shop for supplies at a dollar store.* They have everything from silverware to plastic storage containers to pots and pans — for about a dollar. Sure they won't last forever, but you probably don't want them to.

- *Eat the specials.* Choose a nearby grocery store. Build your menu from their weekly specials or coupon items.

- *Share with friends.* Establish potluck days with friends. Bring containers to split leftovers.

- *Cook ahead and freeze.* Make a full meal (say a chicken or big pot of lentil soup). Freeze single-meal sized portions. This also works for treats like cookies or muffins.

- *Pack a lunch and snacks.* You'll save money and eat healthier foods.

- *Buy a partial meal plan.* If packing a lunch doesn't work for you, explore options to purchase a partial or pay-as-you-go meal plan at the school cafeteria.

- *Find free food.* Attend campus events that advertise free food or "heavy hors d'oeuvres".

- *Drink cheap coffee.* Find the cheap or free coffee on campus. Buy generic brands on sale for home. Save Starbucks for the graduation party.

- *Save the environment.* Buy a water filter and refillable bottle.

- *Shop the dollar menus.* Many fast food places now boast dollar menus. Mix and match. Buy a kids meal and save the toy.

Ramen noodles aren't the only way to save on food.

Transportation

Environmental interests have led cities and colleges to expand local transportation options. Bike and walking trails, intercampus and city buses, subways and light rail provide economical means of travel from home to work or to class. You'll save on parking fees, large repair bills and expensive trips to the gas station. For the occasional interview or large shopping trip, some metropolitan areas offer Hour Cars; cars that can be rented by the hour for a fraction of the cost of ownership.

Explore the options in your area. Pick up bus schedules and bike route maps. Give each a try! The more you know, the better your transportation decisions will be. The best choice this term may be different next term, depending on your class or work schedule and living arrangement. The most common transportation alternatives to a car are:

- *Walk* — Get some fresh air and free exercise by walking wherever you can. Invest in comfortable shoes, weather-appropriate clothes and a decent backpack with wheels (available at low-cost retailers such as Kohl's and Penney's for around $30 on sale). Look up. Notice the sky, birds, and interesting architecture. Even a short walk can give your brain a much-needed break. Remember recess? Recent research shows that kids learn better when they have regular physical activity. Think of yourself as a big kid. Get outside.

- *Bike* — If time is of the essence, bike. Bikes and students go together like pizza and beer. Buy a good lock as well as lights or reflective clothing for night-time trips. Invest in a helmet — don't risk knocking out all your expensive, hard-earned knowledge in one fall.

- *Bus* (intercampus) — Large campuses or college consortiums (e.g., a group of private colleges that work together) typically have an intercampus bus that is free or very low cost. You've paid for it through fees. Use it.

- *Bus* (city) — If you are in a city with a local bus system, take advantage of student discounts on bus passes or individual tickets. If you live far from campus but on a bus route, the trip can be a nice chance to catch up on reading (or sleep).

- *Scooter* — Faster than a bike, easy to park, and cheaper than most cars, scooters are making a comeback on campus. Search for deals on Craig's List.

For long trips, ask for student discounts. Many major air, boat, bus and rail carriers offer special student promotions or discounts on regular fares. Use Google to locate travel groups that specialize in low-cost student trips. If you don't see student discount rates, call and ask.

Travel green to save some green.

Health Care

Student health care is a hot topic, especially for colleges with graduate programs. Recent reports suggest a third or more of graduate students may not take out health coverage under the belief that (a) they are young and healthy, and (b) insurance is a waste of money. This is not wise. A good investor takes steps to protect his investment. Health care is one way to protect your educational investment in you. Be wise.

If you are injured or become seriously ill, the costs associated with your care as an uninsured patient can quickly drain resources earmarked for education. In addition, health care debt is one of the leading causes of bankruptcy — not the kind of stress you need. Think of health care as you think of collision insurance for your car. You want the option to fix your body if damage occurs.

There are three standard choices:

- **Stay on your parents' plan** – This is an option if you are under 26 years of age.

- **Purchase an individual plan** – Several large providers offer low-cost, high-deductible plans for students (e.g., BlueCross BlueShield).

- **Accept the school's plan** – Know what the plan does and does not cover. In some cases it might be possible and appropriate to take this plan AND an individual or parent's plan.

As a student, you may be eligible for certain free or reduced-fee services, such as mental health care, at the student health clinic on campus or a local clinic affiliated with the school whether or not you have insurance.

A large university clinic may include medical, dental, mental health, vision and occasionally integrative therapies. If you are an online student, ask how the college handles health insurance for students. Assume there are resources. Find them and use them.

Finally, people with a health care plan tend to take better care of themselves than the uninsured. Health issues are discovered and treated in early stages because medical attention is sought for the lingering cough or persistent physical complaint. Moreover, people who care for themselves physically, tend to pay attention to mental health needs like taking a walk in the woods, meeting a friend for dinner, or recognizing the difference between short-term stress and long-term anxiety or depression.

Whatever plan you choose, take care of you!

Protect your investment in you.

Life Moves On — Weddings, Babies and Other Expenses

There you were. Single, carefree, happy to live for free in your parent's basement while you attended graduate school. And then things changed. You met the love of your life, planned a wedding, welcomed a surprise baby and had a chance to buy a home at today's rock-bottom prices. Even *one* of these major life events can threaten to derail a student budget. Here are a few tips to keep you sane and financially stable during changing times.

1. *DO NOT USE STUDENT LOANS TO FUND MAJOR LIFE EVENTS.*

   It might seem like a quick fix, but taking on extra student loans to cover non-school bills is an expensive, long-term solution to a short-term challenge Doing so may even violate your contract with the lender if the loan funds are eligible for favorable tax treatment. Approach events from your low-budget, student reality. Otherwise, whenever possible wait until the income is available.

2. *Ask about student discounts everywhere.*

   Many small retailers and service providers offer discounts to students, especially if the business is near campus. If not, seek out less expensive choices that meet your needs.

3. *Shop at garage sales, second-hand or thrift stores.*

Look on coffee shop bulletin boards, Craigs List or garage sales for baby or household items. Shop at second-hand or thrift stores sponsored by a specific non-profit (e.g., Goodwill, Hope Chest, and Arc's Value Village). The quality, selection and deals can be incredible.

4. *Hire a student or new graduate.*

Whether you need a nanny, photographer, caterer, vocalist or designer, consider hiring a student or young artist. My daughter hired a new designer to create and sew a simple, yet elegant wedding dress at a fraction of the cost of off-the-shelf dresses. She hired a gifted high school musician for the ceremony and an emerging young photographer who took amazing pictures. The student or recent grad gets exposure and you get a great price.

5. *Manage expectations.*

Family and guests understand you are a student with no time and a tight budget. Do not exceed those expectations.

You are still a student, with a student's budget, no matter how many life events come along.

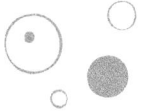

CHAPTER FOUR

Managing Debt

Educational financing is a complex field with ever-changing rules, regulations and programs. The best way to manage debt is to have none. However, that is impractical for most graduate students. The next best thing is to limit debt to where loan payments do not uncomfortably impact post-graduation lifestyle. How do you identify a reasonable debt limit without firm data? Reliable data is essential.

The good news is there is a plethora of resource materials and self-help guides available through financial aid officers, the library, trustworthy websites and annual print resources. The bad news is there is a plethora of resources. Rather than attempt to replicate or replace them, this chapter prepares you to best utilize current resources.

Defining Reasonable

The true measure of "reasonableness" for one's education debt takes place long after graduation. If you landed a great job with long-term opportunities, you will likely declare your investment to have been reasonable. If instead you find yourself deep in debt, struggling to find employment adequate to pay student loans, and asking yourself "what was I thinking", then it is unlikely you will be pleased with the investment.

But, you need to define "reasonable" NOW, before you take on any debt. Without knowing the future, how can increase the likelihood of a happy ending? Fortunately, there are a few tricks to help you get in the reasonable-debt-load ballpark, so to speak.

As a rule of thumb, consider the "reasonable person" perspective from law (not the same as "average" but similar…) Would a reasonable person consider $75,000 in student loans to be a good investment risk to get a Harvard MBA? Based on general knowledge of Harvard grads' financial career success[4], the reasonable person would likely say yes. What about $75,000 for an online Management master's degree program at Never Heard of You U? The same reasonable person would probably ask a lot of questions before making a decision. Find a reasonable person who is detached from your situation; someone with an accurate perspective on the situation who will tell you the truth. Ask for their opinion as you compare programs.

---

4   http://www.forbes.com/lists/2011/95/best-business-schools-11_rank.html

Next, dig into the details with these five questions:

1. *Does this degree[5] warrant the debt?*

   > To answer, you need to know what you truly want from the degree. Personal fulfillment? Career advancement? High salary? Flexible career? Besides asking if the degree warrants the debt, ask yourself if your goal warrants the debt. If it does, move on to the next question. If not, you're done.

2. *Is there a market for this degree?*

   > Do your best to discern whether or not there will be job opportunities in this field by the time you graduate. What are national (or local) job projections for this training? The greater the market demand, the better your chances of landing a job (which means income for loan payments).

3. *What is the market for my institutional brand?*

   > Brand matters. Employers understand what a Harvard or Michigan grad brings to the job. Likewise, name-brand regional schools may carry weight with local employers. The stronger your brand in the job market you hope to enter, the safer your investment in the brand.

---

5   In this question examples of a 'degree' are MBA, PhD in French Literature, Masters in Computer Science, MD with an emphasis in cardiology, and so forth.

The Forbes[6] study cited earlier makes this point. Every other year, Forbes publishes comparative data about individuals who graduated five years ago from top business schools. The report estimates the number of years before the investment pays off for the average student.[7] The data is not based on starting salaries, but salaries 5 *years out*; top B-school grads; with top GMAT scores. If your school is not on this list, assume a lower salary. Borrow accordingly.

4. *What is my current debt load? What will my debt load likely be after graduate school?*

Estimate your total student loan payments after graduation. You will be responsible for minimum payments on each loan. When you read "minimum payments as low as $50 a month", that means per loan. If you have 10 loans (very common) that means $500 if each of them is small enough for a $50/month payment. If you have multiple loans from the same lender, the lender may simplify your life and theirs by adding all your "minimums" up into one monthly payment. But don't expect it to be $50. Several of the resources in Chapter 7 include calculators to estimate total loan payments by type of loan, term and interest rate. Estimating your total monthly payment before

_____

6   http://www.forbes.com/lists/2011/95/best-business-schools-11_rank.html
7 Note: The 5-year-post-graduation average salary ranges from $230k (Harvard) to $71k per year (Auburn).

you choose a school helps you identify a reasonable debt load given factors such as your degree, the market for your degree, the market for your institution's brand, and the last consideration: the lifestyle you want to lead.

5. *What lifestyle do you hope to lead? What personal goals or events do you envision, near-term or long-term?*

Are you engaged and planning a wedding? Do you plan to start a family in the next five years? Buy a new car? A nice house in the suburbs (with matching furniture)? Travel around the world? Does your significant other plan to return to school? Do you? Do you want to save for your children's education (pre-school through college)?

These and other life events take money. The larger your student loan payments are, the less money you'll have available for other things. Plus, defaulting on a student loan can affect your ability to qualify for a car loan or house mortgage.

Life is about balance. Reasonable student debt is debt that takes into account the potential pay-off of the investment (e.g., good-paying career) with the impact of the cost (loan payments) on the life you hope to lead.

When in doubt,
get a detached, reasonable person's opinion.

How is Graduate School Debt Different?

Graduate school debt is somewhat different from under-graduate debt. Understanding the differences and their significance will help you manage graduate school debt.

Graduate school loans are larger.

Loan limits are higher for advanced degrees, to reflect higher tuition and living costs of graduate students. But don't let a lender tell you how much you should borrow. Know what you need, and take no more. Just because you *can* borrow tens of thousands of dollars, doesn't mean you *should*.

More loan programs may be available.

More programs means increased access to graduate school for low-income students. Yet as with multiple credit cards, you can easily lose track of your total debt commitment, let alone what you owe to whom. Track every loan you take, including deferred undergraduate loans. Use a chart that is easy to update, such as the one at the end of this chapter. Never lose track of your total debt obligation.

Loan maximums may be based on outdated assumptions of high salaries.

The operative term is "assumption." Don't assume that if someone is willing to lend you $100,000, the lender believes you will (a) get a job right away and (b) for about $100,000. Not true. Case in point: When new law school grads had their pick of offers starting at $80k or more, borrowing $80k for law school was reasonable. As the job market disappeared, tuition rose while student loan limits expanded to meet the (institution's) cost. Borrowing is your decision, but remember: you are responsible for loan payments whether you are making $100k, $10k or $0k. Borrow with the job market in mind.

Loans are due sooner.

Undergraduate students often start thinking (worrying) about loan payments during their junior or senior year — when there is still time to pull together a plan. The majority of graduate programs take two years full-time to complete.[8] Some are shorter. Graduate students who borrow without a plan find themselves facing loan payments before they have a chance to put away their books.

Loan deferment for further education is limited.

Unemployed and worried about her soon-due undergrad loan payments, Siri enrolls in a master's program. Whether this is a wise choice aside, Siri *has* this choice. Once she earns her master's she must face her accumulated loan payments — unless she pursues more education. And incurring even more debt is only a good idea if the education is essential for a long-term career plan.

> *Choose student loans based on your needs,*
> *not on loan availability.*

---

8 Alternatively, JD, PhD or MD students may lose track of their total loan debt as graduation seems so far away.

Loan Refresher

Student loans are essential to the American higher education system. Unwieldy loan payments can become a financial burden, however. Wise choices start with an understanding of one's basic options. Even if you took undergraduate student loans, skim this section to refresh your memory.

There are three basic types of student loans:

Federal Loans

Following passage of the Health Education Reconciliation Act of 2010, the Federal Direct Loan Program became the sole government-back student loan program. Funded through taxpayer dollars, *Direct Loans* typically offer the lowest interest rates and flexible payback options, such as deferment and forbearance. *Always take federal loans first.* Plus, programs such as the Public Service Loan Forgiveness Program and the Stafford Loan Forgiveness Program for Teachers only apply to federal loans.

The U.S. Department of Education website contains excellent information about graduate and professional school aid.[9] Many but not all educational institutions or programs qualify to receive federal student loan funds. Repayment generally begins six months following graduation or when you fall below half-time status. Read the promissory note and check with the financial aid office for details.

---

9   http://studentaid.ed.gov/PORTALSWebApp/students/english/gradstudent.jsp

Private Student Loans

Private loans come from lending agencies (e.g., Access Group) and banks. Private loans may require a co-signature[10]. A few may be available through your school, your state, a professional organization or school affiliation. Occasionally, large companies such as Dell offer special credit plans to students to purchase the company's product. Private loans typically have higher interest rates than federal loans, may require minimum payments during school or immediately upon graduation (or less than half-time status), do not qualify for government forgiveness programs, and have minimal hardship options.

Really Private Student Loans

You probably don't think of these as loans as they come directly from a personal connection. Typically this means relatives. Arrangements may be formal (signed agreement — preferable in any situation) or informal (handshake — leaves room for misunderstanding). Amounts may be minimal or truly significant. Payback may be expected in cash or through an alternative arrangement. For example, one large immigrant family took turns funding each other's education. All six children earned professional degrees and the family thrived. If you borrow from a friend or relative, make certain you understand each other's expectations and the agreed-upon payment terms (including interest).

What type of loans do you have?

---

10 Be VERY cautious with co-signatures. Co-signers are on the hook if you fail to repay the loan. Co-signing may also affect their ability to borrow for major purchases such as a house or car.

Old Loans

Few students are debt-free when they start graduate school. Some debt can be deferred while you pursue your next degree. Other debt (e.g., credit cards) cannot be deferred. Speak to each lender to identify options available to you. Know the consequences of each choice. A short-term deferment might be a great quick-fix, but understand the rules as well as the cost.

Undergraduate federal loans

Students attending approved graduate programs at least half time may defer undergraduate loan payments. Consider paying accrued interest quarterly to keep total debt down and avoid paying interest on interest. Ask the financial aid office, or go to the Department of Education website for forms.[11]

Undergraduate private loans

Contact the lender (typically a bank). Explore options. Even if deferment is not possible, you may be able to negotiate a temporarily reduced payment while you are in graduate school. Ask about fees, penalties and rules before making a final decision. Each lender is different.

Undergraduate personal loans

These are loans from friends, family or personal affiliations (e.g., an education loan awarded by a local non-profit). Approach each lender with your plans and specific request. Expect to pay something extra for the lender to wait another two years or so to get his/her money back. Be respectful and grateful for their past

11 At www.dl.ed.gov Search for "deferment forms" and "deferment lists".

generosity. Gracefully accept "no," if they must stick to your original deal.

Credit card debt

Do everything you possibly can to start graduate school free of credit card debt. Take an extra job delivering pizzas for a summer. Hold a garage sale with stuff from high school and college you no longer use. Save, save, save — and apply every penny to pay off your credit cards. Not only will you have more money available for grad school expenses, you'll discover what you really need and what you can live without — at least for now. Keep one credit card to use for emergencies. Pay it in full each month.

Make a plan for old loans first.

New Loans

Graduate school federal loans fall into two categories: Direct Stafford loans and Direct PLUS loans. Links to information about each are below. Additional financial aid websites are described in Chapter 7, *Resources*. Explore each of these sites. Compare information.

As you learned earlier, take federal loans first to get the best interest rates and multiple payback options. Unlike federal undergraduate loans which have low loan limits, the Direct PLUS loan for graduate students covers all costs of attendance less other aid received up to $20,500 per year or an aggregate amount of $138,500. Thus, for many graduate students there should be no need to borrow private loans. Students in certain health professions may be eligible for federal aid up to $47,167 per year with an aggregate limit of $224,000.[12]

Set a debt ceiling for completion of your program. Discuss options with your financial aid officer or another graduate student loan expert. Sketch out a plan through graduation. Stick with your plan — or at least know when you veer from it and why.

Bookmark these two resources:

+ **U.S. Department of Education:** The Federal Student Aid[13] division administers the Direct

---

12 http://ifap.ed.gov/dpcletters/041808GEN0804.html
13   http://studentaid.ed.gov/PORTALSWebApp/students/english/index.jsp

PLUS[14] loans and Direct Stafford[15] loans for graduate and professional degree students. Each year they distribute more than $150 billion in aid to more than 14 million post-secondary students.

+ **FinAid.org** is the most highly respected, thorough financial aid website. Example pages include:

    + Data on **average loan debt** by level of degree[16]

    + A Private Student Loan comparison chart that lists all lenders with links to their sites/loan apps.[17] Note: FinAid lists all lenders whereas other private loan sites only list those that pay to participate.

    + Info and links to the resources for **scholarships and fellowships**.[18]

In addition to standard federal and private loans, some lenders offer specific loans for high-cost professional programs (e.g., law and medicine). Compare details such as interest rates (fixed or variable), consolidation options, and eligibility for forgiveness or debt reduction initiatives. Choose carefully and you could save thousands of dollars over the life of the loans.

---

14   http://studentaid.ed.gov/PORTALSWebApp/students/english/PlusLoansGradProfstudents.jsp
15   http://studentaid.ed.gov/PORTALSWebApp/students/english/studentloans.jsp
16 http://www.finaid.org/loans/
17 http://www.finaid.org/loans/privatestudentloans.phtml
18 http://www.finaid.org/scholarships/

Politics and Grad Loans

The big news in 2011 was the elimination of federal subsidies for graduate student loans, beginning in 2012. Undergraduate students can still qualify for subsidized federal loans. If you received a federally subsidized loan as an undergrad, the government paid the interest on your loan while you were in school and during grace or deferment periods (such as now, perhaps.)

Prior to this ruling, graduate students who qualified could also borrow a certain amount of federal money that was subsidized by the government (taxpayer dollars) and another chunk that was not subsidized (aka "unsubsidized federal loans"). Not any more. Over the next ten years, $125 billion in subsidized loan volume for graduate students will shift to unsubsidized funds. The cuts saved Pell Grants for 8 million undergraduate students, but the estimated 10-year cost to graduate students is $18 million. I'll explain.

The price you pay for a loan is the *total interest* plus any fees. Interest begins *accruing* (adding up) when the money is disbursed to you. Student loan providers typically *defer* (delay) payments while the student is studying at least half time. However, the interest associated with that loan accrues.

Without the subsidy, interest accrues and compounds over time. Thus the $5,000 loan you borrow your first year of grad school could have a much higher balance by the time you graduate. It is estimated that those hardest hit (medical, law and humanities and social science PhD students) could owe an additional $20,000 over the life of their loans.

Thus, to summarize: Beginning with loans for enrollment periods on or after July 1, 2012 federal loan funds earmarked for subsidized loans will become <u>unsubsidized.</u> The federal loan funds will still be available; but the government will no longer pay the interest for you on the portion of your loans they used to subsidize. Instead, the interest will accrue while you are in school - unless you pay it along the way.

Subsidy elimination for graduate loans is a good example of the role of politics in higher education. Be informed. Join a campus advocacy group. Read about current issues. Vote.

Set a debt ceiling when you begin.
Design a budget to match.

I'm Deep in Debt — What Now?!

What if you're already in graduate school and worried about debt. What can you do to mitigate costs and complete your program? **Start now.** Adopt a "no-spending" mindset. If you are already deep in debt, you probably feel overwhelmed. Sometimes simply knowing where you stand helps. Try this:

Note: The color-coding scheme is intended be helpful and fun. If you hate color-coding, ignore it.

Assess your student loan debt.

List your outstanding student loans using the chart at the end of this chapter. Include loans in deferral and personal student loans. Calculate the total balance. Circle that number in **red** — for "stop." Calculate the total of the minimum monthly payments as if all of those payment were due today. Circle that number in **green** — for "this is how much you owe each month."

List your monthly expenses.

Review your checkbook or debit card for last month to see where and how much you really spend. Once the shock wears off, build a short-term survival budget that is workable for the remainder of your graduate program (include housing, food, health care, transportation, basic needs). Circle this number in **blue** — for "this is one sad budget".

Look for ways to cut expenses. Sell the car and get a bike. Shop with coupons. Drop the gym membership and take up jogging. Remind yourself this is a short-term choice.

Clarify remaining school expenses.

Estimate charges for tuition, fees, books and anything else you need to graduate. <u>Circle this number in **yellow**</u>, for "Caution." Funds you take in additional loans to cover these expenses must be added to the number circled earlier in <u>red</u> (total loan debt) and the number circled earlier in <u>green</u> (total monthly loan payments). Your goal is to keep this number as low as possible.

Revive your search for funding.

Ask professors, financial aid officers and other students for leads to scholarships and grants,[19] assistantships or part-time work. A few private foundations, especially those tied directly to your school (e.g., alumni-funded scholarships) prefer to help those beyond the first year or more of a graduate program. Any funds awarded reduce your <u>yellow</u> number (cost to complete the program) and keep a lid on the <u>red</u> number (total loan debt incurred). Both are good things.

Likewise, more part-time jobs are available to students with coursework under their belt. Talk to everyone in career services. Speak to your advisor. Have coffee with the Dean, program director or anyone else who seems to "know" things and be well networked. Ask a favorite professor if he/she needs a teaching or research assistant. Connect with alums. Deliver pizza if you must.

Track your monthly earnings. <u>Circle this number in **orange**</u> — for "soon I can lie in the sun on a hot beach with the money I'm saving by earning funds rather than

---

19 Fastweb.com offers an extensive database of scholarships and grants including many for graduate students.

taking out more student loans" (ok…you may want to shorten that up, but you get the idea). Consider setting and earnings goal that will cover your monthly living expenses — the number circled earlier in blue. The closer the orange number is to the blue number (earnings versus expenses), the sooner you'll be on the beach.

Assess other debt.

Make a separate chart for credit card or non-school personal debt (e.g., dentist or vet bill, car payment) List each debt, payment due date, current balance, interest rate and minimum payment. Order them from highest to lowest balance or highest to lowest interest rate (whichever you prefer). Stop using credit cards for convenience. Use them only as back-up funds for true emergencies.

Make minimum payments unless you can pay them off. Do **not** pay off non-school bills with student loan money! If you run out of funds you could jeopardize your education — and find yourself facing student loan payments far sooner than planned.

If you have multiple bills, try the "snowball technique" promoted by personal financial management experts as a proven method to get out of debt. When the first bill is paid off, add the minimum amount you were paying on that bill to the next bill in line (ranked by highest interest rate or by lowest balance — your choice). Keep going until you are debt free.

Create a plan.

Map out the months from now until graduation (aka, the light at end of the tunnel). Track your progress.

Forgive minor indiscretions. Plan a (reasonably priced) post-graduation celebration.

For easy analysis, copy your numbers here:

Red – Total student loan debt today

$ _____

Green – Total of the minimum monthly payments for student loans already incurred

$ _____

Yellow – Estimated school-related cost to complete graduate program

$ _____

Blue – Personal monthly living expense budget

$ _____

Orange – Monthly earnings (today)

$ _____

Start Today

Repaying Graduate School Debt

Loans must be repaid, period. Except in very rare circumstances, both federal and private student loans are not dischargeable in bankruptcy. Standard repayment terms for graduate school loans range from 10-25 years. When choosing a lender ask what repayment options are available for each loan. Inquire about **deferment, forbearance**[20], **income-based repayment plans**[21], **consolidation**[22], and even **loan cancellation**[23] or **forgiveness**[24] options. Some repayment options only apply to federal loans. Ask each lender about options and read the promissory note.

Some repayment programs are tied to certain fields such as teaching or public service. For example, the Public Service Loan Forgiveness[25] program is a debt-management program that discharges remaining debt on eligible loans after 10 years of public service (given you meet additional criteria). The Stafford Loan Forgiveness for Teachers[26] applies to those who teach in a low-income area for five consecutive years. Review eligibility details, particularly if you have a co-signer or a mix of federal and private loans. Ask an expert for guidance. Finaid. com and AskHeatherJarvis.com are exceptional.

---

20 http://www.nolo.com/legal-encyclopedia/student-loans-cancellation-deferment-forbearance-29791.html
21 http://www.ibrinfo.org/
22 https://loanconsolidation.ed.gov/AppEntry/apply-online/appindex.jsp (includes info on IBR)
23 http://studentaid.ed.gov/PORTALSWebApp/students/english/teachercancel.jsp?tab=funding (teacher program)
24 http://www.finaid.org/loans/forgiveness.phtml
25 http://www.finaid.org/loans/publicservice.phtml
26 http://studentaid.ed.gov/PORTALSWebApp/students/english/teachercancel.jsp?tab=funding

If you are already in repayment, check with your lender(s) to determine current repayment plans available for each loan. The **Project on Student Debt**[27] and **Student Loan Borrowers Assistance**[28] describe common options and offer links to helpful resources. If your loan debt is too high to manage[29], contact your lender(s) BEFORE missing a payment. Calling the lender early demonstrates your intent to find a workable solution to repay the loan.

A few simple steps can help you avoid a debt crisis during repayment.

1. Know the cost for the program before you sign up. You wouldn't buy a car before you knew the price. Use the same judgment for school.

2. Know how much debt is reasonable for this degree (and this institution).[30]

3. Use federal loans. Use private loans cautiously and sparingly.

4. Use loan money only for its intended purpose.

5. Be fiscally conservative but not cheap. Buy the supplies and books you need. Take advantage of

---

27 http://projectonstudentdebt.org/about.vp.html
28 http://www.studentloanborrowerassistance.org/
29 http://www.finaid.org/loans/troublerepayingdebt.phtml
30 Forbes publishes comparative data about recent graduates from top business schools, including an estimate of years-to-payback (tuition) for each school. Note: The 5-year-post-graduation average salary ranges from $230k to $71k per year. This is 5 years out; top B-schools; top GMAT scores. If your school is not on this list, assume a lower salary. Borrow accordingly. http://www.forbes.com/lists/2011/95/best-business-schools-11_rank.html

important opportunities, especially those that may not be available to you after graduation.

6. Set a debt limit for school before you begin. Keep track of your progress.

7. Track your loans each term using a simple chart such as the model at the end of this chapter.

Know your options before times get tough.

Common Mistakes

The most common, preventable, student-loan mistakes occur when graduate students:

- *Succumb to Monopoly-money brain.* This occurs when student loan funds no longer feel like real money.

    - Warning sign: You hear yourself saying, "What's another hundred bucks?"

- *Use loan funds for non-school expenses.* Student loans are for tuition, fees, student-style housing and minimum daily expenses (such as low-budget meals and dollar-store shampoo).

    - Warning sign: "If I take out the maximum loan we can buy a second car (or pay for the wedding, or go on a cruise)."

- *Fail to take time to understand loan details.* The difference between total payments over the life of a federal loan versus a private loan for the same amount can be tens of thousands of dollars. Likewise, certain loans are eligible for income-based repayment plans and government-sponsored forgiveness programs. Others are not.

    - Warning sign: "Just show me where to sign."

- *Fail to track loan debt.* In the hustle and stress of graduate school, it is easy to lose track of how much you've borrowed unless you pay careful attention each term. The best way to graduate

with reasonable debt is to know where you stand
every step of the way.

- Warning sign: "I'm too busy to figure out
  how much I owe in loans. I'll worry about it
  after graduation."

*Live like a student while you ARE a student
so you don't have to later.*

Student Loan Tracking Form

Use the form on the next page to keep a running tally of how much you have committed to repay.[31]

1.   Complete this form including ALL outstanding undergraduate loans — even if deferred.

2.   Each term, add any new graduate loans.

3.   Keep your eye on total debt owed.

Given careful planning, student loans don't have to be a burden. For many, they are a blessing. As one international graduate student said, "I love your country! Your government says, 'Here is money for school. Go. Learn. Better yourself. Then pay us back so someone else can go.' Americans are so lucky!"

---

31 A free downloadable version you can customized is available at http://www.backtoschoolforgrownups.com

Student Loan Tracking Form

Name of Lender	Federal or Private Loan	Loan Amount	Date Taken	Minimum Payment (monthly)	Interest Rate	Term (yrs.)	Loan Servicer Contact Info	1st Pmt Due
	Total debt owed=		Running total monthly payments=					

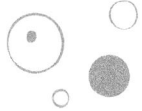

CHAPTER FIVE

Getting Hired

Whether you graduate with student loans or debt-free, the next step for most graduates in the "was it worth it" equation is getting hired in their new field. Getting hired comes down to six things:

1. *Opportunity*. Does a job opening exist?

2. *Awareness*: Do you know about the opportunity?

3. *Qualifications*: Do you qualify on paper?

4. *Credibility*: Do you appear to be who you say you are (in your resume, interview and through references)?

5. *Fit*: Do you feel (to the employer) like a "fit" for the culture, team or key projects?

6. *Choice*: Are you the right employee for them? Is this the right job for you?

Opportunities come and go. Qualifications are built through education and work experience. "Fit" is the squishy part of this equation, and choice is individual by definition. That leaves awareness and credibility. *Chapter Five shows you how to uncover opportunities and build credibility* — and gather work experience and a sense of "fit" in the process.

Stuff to Do Before Graduate School

Pre-Volunteer

Test-drive your interest in a specific career by volunteering in the field. In the process you'll gain an inside view to the actual work professionals do as well as the type of people who make this their life's work.

Write about your volunteer experience in your entrance essay. Ask for a reference from your team leader or from the organization's highest ranking person who knows your work. You'll gain credibility with admissions and future employers as someone with insight and respect for the field. And you may meet a future boss.

Engage Your References

Don't just send an email to favorite professors requesting a recommendation for graduate school. Meet with them. Share your vision for your graduate degree. Ask their advice and what they know about the job market. Ask if they could introduce you to two or three top-notch professionals in the field. Keep in touch while you are in school.

Write a Paper or Blog Piece

Choose a topic of interest to you that relates to your prospective field. Keep the topic narrow but intriguing, such as (1) the effect of annual geese migration on small towns in Iowa, (2) elements of an effective retail training program for seasonal employees, or (3) five community-building activities for kids in high-turnover K-3 bilingual classrooms. You never know when your work might appear in someone's Google search.

Lay a foundation early for your job search.

Stuff to Do During Graduate School

Look for an Internship in Your Field of Interest

Competition for internships can be fierce. Be creative. Big companies have internship rules that must be followed. Small shops may just need to get the work done. What small employer may need someone with your expertise short-term (for free or low-cost)? When you see a business that needs what you do, send a proposal. Initiative is a good thing.

Look for an Internship or Part-time Job With Your First-Choice Employer

Even if you sort mail, time with your first-choice employer is time on site. Every day is an opportunity to meet future colleagues and hiring managers. Watch for job ads on the company intranet. When you see a job you'd like, express your interest to the hiring manager. You'll be the first to learn about internships. And if you are hired full-time, you may even be eligible for tuition reimbursement.

Join a Professional Organization

Find the local and national chapters of the leading professional organization(s) in your field. Examples include the American Bar Association, Society for Human Resource Management, and the National Science Teachers Association. Become familiar with their websites. Review job postings for entry-level requirements. See who is hiring. Notice what titles (and qualifications) describe the job you want after graduation.

Attend Professional Conferences

Student discounts and volunteer opportunities make conference attendance affordable for the average student. Local conferences introduce you to a local market; national conferences often host a job board with openings around the globe. Write down the contact information for jobs of interest, or with companies where you'd like to work. Make contact when you begin your search. As a student you can play the "I'm a student researching my options" card, which can open some doors. Mention where and when you saw the posting; ask if a similar position is available now or will be in the future.

Develop Campus Relationships

Get to know the administration, faculty and career services office. Each of these individuals is likely to hear about job openings through their personal and professional connections. Ask for two or three referrals to alums or other professionals in your field. Follow up, and then send thank you notes to the new contact as well as to the individual making the reference.

Build professional relationships while you are in school.

Stuff to Do After Graduate School

Things to do if you DON'T have a job when you graduate

+ Understand the status of your loans – When do payments begin? How much will they be? Is interest accruing that you could pay down?

+ Identify loan payment options you may want or need to invoke[32], such as:

    + Consolidation (make sure it won't affect other options you want available, such as participation in federal loan forgiveness or cancellation programs)

    + Income Based Repayment

    + Deferral

    + Forbearance

+ Assess your work options – Will you need to move to a different city (or country)? Re-evaluate salary and job title requirements. Volunteer for a cause you support. You'll get experience, make contacts and boost your confidence while helping someone else.

+ Assess your living options – Balance cheap options (e.g., living with family) with practical considerations such as family relationships and proximity to potential work.

+ Take a part-time hourly job – You'll earn a few bucks, continue to meet people and have something to put on your resume.

---

32 Read more about each of these in Chapter Four, *Managing Debt*.

- Reconnect with past networking contacts – Let them know you've graduated. Thank them for their support in the past. Ask them for one suggestion for your job search. Share your resume. Be positive. Do NOT complain.

- Reconnect with graduate school references – Stay in touch. Thank them for their ongoing support. Be specific. These people have a vested interest in your success. Ask about their strategy for landing their first job. Ask what they believe is most important in a job search. Thank them again.

Things to do if you DO have a job when you graduate

- Contact your network – faculty, internship supervisor, classmates, friends and family. Let them know where you landed, what you'll be doing, and how to contact you. Thank them for their part in getting you there. Keep in touch.

Be positive. Do something.

Stuff to Do Throughout Your Career

Actively connect with your alumni association(s)

Join your undergraduate and graduate alumni associations. Stay in touch through in-person gatherings, the alumni LinkedIn groups or other social media.

Join your professional association

Attend meetings. Be upbeat and energetic. Listen to the pros. Always carry copies of your resume and business cards.

Comment on blog articles

Get your name out in the community. When you see an interesting article or blog post, add a comment. Contact the author, or at least review their professional website and LinkedIn profile. Where have they worked? What can you learn about their career path from their LinkedIn profile? Roaming around the Internet is a great way to discover companies and jobs you didn't know existed.

A word about social media

Stay in front of your professional contacts through professional forms of social media. Keep in mind that anything you post on the Internet, even on personal sites such as Facebook, may end up in front of a recruiter, colleague or supervisor. Choose your words and photos carefully.

And if you only have time for one activity:

NETWORK

*Jobs come and jobs go
but networking goes on forever.*

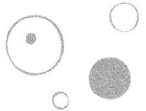

CHAPTER SIX

How I Minimized Student Debt

Nine individuals share their best cost-saving tips and strategies for graduate school in this chapter. As of this publication six writers had graduated, two were finishing school and one was weighing pros and cons for his final plan.

True Stories

It has been said, if you want to know how to do something, ask someone who has done it (or who is doing it now). Each story in this chapter was written by such an expert.

The writers represent nine fields of study:

- Educational Psychology/International Studies
- Creative Writing
- Law
- Public Health Policy
- Anthropology
- K-8 Bilingual Education
- Divinity/Social Justice
- Medicine
- Vocal Performance

The writers were asked to share their best tips for mitigating graduate school expenses. The following questions were provided as a framework. However, writers were free to share their story however they wished. Creativity was encouraged.

1. **The 1-3 best thing(s) I did up front (before choosing a program or school) to control graduate school expenses were...** Did cost factor into your decision about what to study, where to go or what to look for in a school (such as good job placement rates, flexible program that

allowed you to work, fellowship opportunities, something else?)

2. **The 1-3 best thing(s) I did during graduate school to control expenses and debt were...** What cost-saving strategies are you most proud of? That worked out well for you? These can be small (saved $$$ by buying generic, riding my bike, sharing books) or big (attended 3rd choice school that provided full tuition).

3. **What would I do differently?** Looking back, is there anything you wish you would have "splurged" on (study abroad, working less or doing an unpaid internship)? Places where you could have saved? Where would I spend more? Where would I spend less?

4. **Inspiration.** Please include (and cite the author) any favorite inspirational phrase, motto or image that kept you going through difficult times.

The stories are presented as they were submitted by each author, with the exception of minor edits. As such, each writer's voice can be heard through his or her own words. First name and last initial are given — or pen names, when requested by the writer — to maintain a minimal level of anonymity. Likewise, school names were optional. Enjoy!

Tanya G: Make Your Own Beer

Undergraduate Degree: French and International Studies – Kalamazoo College

Graduate Degree: M.A. Educational Psychology

Graduate School: University of Minnesota, Duluth

Current Position: Director of Education at Intercultural Student Experiences

My undergraduate degree is a B.S. in French and International Studies from Kalamazoo College, Kalamazoo, MI. I took 2 years off between my undergrad degree and grad school. I worked three jobs in that two year period in various human services positions and taught after-school extracurricular French.

What are the best things you did up front to control the cost of graduate school?

The best decision that I made in considering what to study in grad school was to listen to people who I worked with and studied with about what I was good at. When you're in your 20's, sometimes you think you know what you want to do; but is it something you would be *good* at?

It is key to consider your own interests and passions but balance that with your talent and skills. I was lucky to have great people in my life who gave me awesome feedback regarding my strengths.

What are the best things you did to control your graduate school cost during school?

To control expenses in grad school, I had at least three things that I'm VERY happy I did to control debt. Here are my favorite three:

1. I was a Teacher's Assistant which gave me extra money to pay bills and helped me to reduce the amount of student loan money I spent on living expenses. This not only gave me great experience in teaching and developing skills like public speaking but it also helped me to decide if I would set my next goal at getting a PhD or getting employment after graduation.

2. I lived modestly in a one-room attic efficiency with a shared bathroom and did not own a credit card. I kept my eye on the prize and anticipated that I would be happy for a day if I got a better apartment or the latest fashion trend, but I'd be VERY happy if I kept my post grad debt down so I could pay it off faster and not be under pressure to unrealistically try to find a high paying dream job just after graduating.

3. I dated someone who made their own beer — huge savings for sure! In order to share in the fruits of his labor and not feel guilty, I did put some work equity into bottling it. As it turned out, that was a great lesson on collaboration to get a job done. I think there is a quote for this: "A job worth doing is worth doing together." — anonymous

What would you do differently?

Seriously, I don't think I would do anything differently.

Did you have a favorite inspiration phrase to get you through?

I did not have an inspirational phrase in grad school to get me through hard times. I'm one of those people who is honestly content to accept situations as they are. It has always served me well to look for opportunity in situations I don't immediately recognize as worthwhile and to be patient when it comes to reaping the rewards from education.

One thing I have always done and still do today when things get tough is to check my perspective by considering what a real trauma or problem would be if I lived in a different time, place or society. As an example from current day — even my lowest days can't compare to what we are seeing in Somalia with all the drought, starvation and lack of functioning government.

Tristan P.: Creative Options

Undergraduate Degree: Public History

Graduate Degree: Creative Writing

Current Position: Museum Exhibit Developer

The best things I did before choosing a program or school to control graduate school expenses were...

I read up on all the programs' schedules and locations. I hadn't thought about doing a low-residency or part-time program until I realized how many excellent ones there were in my field. Because I didn't have to move to a more expensive city or quit my job, that money goes toward tuition.

The best things I did during graduate school to control expenses and debt were...

I use inter-library loan for all my books. My library will order books for me from all over the state, so I only have to buy the books I want to keep.

I've been using my five-year-old laptop, which is on its last legs. I had an impulse to buy a new one for grad school, but I'm waiting until this one gives out on me so that money can go toward tuition, and reduce my loans.

What would I do differently?

I would give more serious effort to seeking out independent scholarships. I won't be making much more money when I finish school, so reducing my loans while I still can is a goal.

Inspiration. What favorite inspirational phrase, motto or image kept you going through difficult times?

"You do not have to be good." —Mary Oliver

I put this quote over my desk to remind myself that it's okay if I feel like I'm doing badly sometimes. I'm not in grad school to be good at everything, I'm in it to make mistakes and learn from them.

Jennifer R.: Planning Ahead

Undergraduate Degree: Bachelor of Science in Legal Studies – University of Wisconsin, Superior

Graduate Degree: Juris Doctor

Graduate School: William Mitchell College of Law

Current Position: Document Review Team Manager

The best things I did before choosing a program control graduate school expenses were...

I attended the Law School Forum in Chicago, IL the two Falls prior to starting law school to gather information about the various schools located in the Twin Cities and the Mid-West region where I wanted to stay. The Law School Forum was a two-day fair with admission representatives from all over the continent and seminars targeting taking the LSAT and financing a law school education.

The first year I went to scope out all of the schools I had to choose from and got information on my favorites admissions requirements so I could make sure I met them with my last year of undergrad studies and LSAT prep courses. The second year I went to narrow my top choices down to three, speak to their admissions personnel directly and get information on financing options, handling the transition to a law program and a variety of other seminar topics related to getting a J.D.

The best things I did during graduate school to control expenses and debt were...

I lived at home with my parents to cut out the costs of rent, utilities and food. This allowed me to take out smaller private loans to cover tuition and book expenses in excess of my Stafford loans. It also allowed me to avoid roommate drama and stress for what could possibly be considered the longest three years of my life to date.

I also only borrowed the amount of money that I needed to cover my necessary educational expenses. I resisted the common urge to take out larger private loans each year just to have "play money" that would have allowed me to not work, live above my means or take Winter/Spring break vacations.

I bought gently used books and study materials when possible. I joined a peer study group, which allowed me to share the financial and time costs of buying or creating study materials with 3-4 others.

What would I do differently?

I would have applied for a paralegal position during the year break I took between undergraduate and law school to get better perspective on why I wanted a J.D. or what I would do with a J.D. My B.S. degree had a paralegal certificate built into it, which I received but never fully leveraged. The possibilities with how this would have impacted my educational course are significant: I may have never gone to law school (thus had zero student loan debt) or I would have gone to law school having learned skills that you need in legal practice but do not learn well or at all in law school. This latter point would have made me more marketable in a legal marketplace that was spiraling down at graduation time.

I would have listened to my parents and not purchased a new car before starting law school. I could have used the payments to avoid taking some of the private student loans I still have 8 years later. Sadly the car did not last longer than those private loans have.

Jacqueline S.: Teach Your Way Through School

Undergraduate Degree: English – Luther College

Graduate Degree: Public Health

Graduate School: University of Michigan School of Public Health

Current Position: Writer

The best things I did before choosing a program or school to control graduate school expenses were...

I used my offer from one university to negotiate more money at another. It didn't get me equal amounts at each but it helped secure more funding.

Cost didn't factor into where I went (but it should have). I chose based on rankings and went to the #4 school in the country.

The best things I did during graduate school to control expenses and debt were...

I walked or biked everywhere. We had one car between my husband and me.

I applied for scholarships while I was in school and got two! You never know unless you apply!

I also applied and received funding to spend 10 weeks in India for an internship.

The biggest thing though I immediately started searching for a graduate student instructor position upon arriving. I got two positions (for both terms my second year). These positions not only paid for my tuition and health insurance, they provided a nice stipend. This made up for the first year, in which we took out loans *and* made out-of-pocket payments.

What would I do differently?

The hardest part was that my husband was unemployed for a few months when we moved. Had we known, I probably would have chosen a different school in Los Angeles where the job market was better for him. I'd say if you have a partner, make sure he/she finds something decent before you move! Unemployment is terrible for morale.

Kate A.: *Explore the World*

Undergraduate Degree: Cultural Anthropology – University of Minnesota, Twin Cities

Graduate Degree: Master of Arts in Anthropology-Sociology

Graduate School: American University in Cairo

Current Position: College Instructor

The story of my graduate school experience begins in my undergraduate years. It was between my sophomore and junior year I decided to study abroad. Actually, I had originally planned to do summer courses locally, at my college, the University of Minnesota. I friend of mine told me she was planning on taking some summer courses at the American University in Cairo. She was Egyptian-American. She had traveled to visit family in Egypt every summer and was familiar with the American University and had already found that credit was transferable. She asked me if I wanted to come too. So, having been long infected with the travel bug and privy to the wisdom that one's best chance to travel is when they are young, I jumped at the chance.

The summer study abroad session in Cairo exposed me to the history and culture of contemporary Egypt. I became familiar with the ideological debates and social issues underway in an intimate, up-close-and-personal manner. It was a first-hand global experience. I met researchers doing field work. I loved it. But three months was not enough. So when I decided to go to graduate school, I chose to return to the American University in Cairo.

This fit me and was a good decision in many ways. Firstly, I had been to Egypt before. I knew a basic lay of the terrain. I could somewhat predict what life would be like in a different country. More importantly, I was familiar with the university environment. Having not had the best grades as an undergraduate (because I worked nearly fulltime), I knew I would still be able to get into the graduate program which was less competitive than some in the United States. Hence, I was able to win three different fellowship awards during my graduate studies.

However my fellowships did not come until my later semesters. The first year, I worked as a Teaching Assistant. The meager salary at least covered my rent which was less than two hundred dollars per month. The low cost of living in Cairo meant that I could fully devote all my time to studying, a luxury I would not have had back at home.

Had I stayed at home, I'd have had to worry about all of the usual financial stressors, the cell phone payment, car insurance, fuel, required gift-giving. In Cairo at the time, it was possible to live quite well for $300-$400 dollars a month (most Egyptians live on much less). Taxis were very inexpensive, school covered health insurance, and in Egypt you only pay for what you use on a cell phone. I needed very little of my student loan to cover living expenses. I would not have been able to do the same had I studied in a stateside university.

Lastly, my major was a significant factor in choosing graduate school. Cultural Anthropology was my passion. American University in Cairo had an Anthropology-Sociology program — close enough for me. Though I did not know much about sociology, I thought it could become a benefit to have this dual credential (and it definitely has been).

Aside from those "native anthropologists" who study their own culture, usually students of anthropology must seek out research grants to go off to the field. By studying in Egypt, I removed another obstacle /financial burden; I was right there, in a research-rich environment I could access without it costing time or money.

By earning my master's degree at American University in Cairo, I saved thousands on the cost of living, and I earned a respected degree that has provided global experience and opened many professional opportunities. Attesting to this is the publication of my master's thesis. Currently I work as a college instructor.

To summarize, I got the education I wanted for the right price because I:

- Took a risk
- Worked as a Teaching Assistant
- Lived thriftily (studied hard!)
- Stayed on track (followed course sequence without breaks)

Tony L.: Choose Your Goals

Undergraduate Degree: Economics and Latin American Studies – Hobart and William Smith Colleges

Graduate Degree: K-8 Education

Graduate School: Hamline University

Current Position: First grade Bilingual Teacher

The best things I did before choosing a program or school to control graduate school expenses were…

I made sure the program I was entering would allow me to continue to work full time. As I had just become a year-round bicycle commuter, I got rid of my car and put as much money as I could into class to avoid taking out significant loans. I ended up taking out loans for about half of my classes.

I also spent time volunteering, working, visiting, and, most importantly, teaching in schools before deciding what area to enter. I was on the fence about teaching high school or elementary. I would be lying if I said the number of credits needed for each did not factor in my decision.

The best things I did during graduate school to control expenses and debt were…

While in school, I shared textbooks with friends, checked some out at the library, and sold many of them online afterward.

After my first semester working toward my teaching degree, I found out that there was a Bilingual Cohort in my district taking classes — fully paid — toward a bilingual certificate. It doubled my class load, but I hopped on that train as fast as I could. This turned out to be the best decision I made regarding grad school.

I finished my teaching degree at the same time I was finishing my bilingual certificate. This not only landed me a job sooner, it increased my beginning salary. Such teachers were so high in demand that I was able to teach on a variance before finishing my teaching degree. I was able to convince my advisor to let me do my student teaching in my own classroom, thus avoiding the "semester without pay" that most soon-to-be-teachers face. I got lucky, really.

A personal choice…

When I started teaching, I had not finished my Masters. Given my credits earned at the graduate level and our latest contract agreement, I had to decide if finishing my Masters at that point was going to make fiscal sense. It's been four years and I still haven't been able to justify taking those final two classes to earn my Masters. Had I finishing my Masters right away, I would now be at the exact same salary, I would be out $4,000, and my gardening skills certainly would not have improved so quickly.

Alison K.: Managing in NYC

Undergraduate Degree: B.A. Spanish Language and Literature – Luther College

Graduate Degree: Master of Divinity

Graduate School: Union Theological Seminary in the City of New York

Current Position: Statewide Organizer at the Joint Religious Legislative Coalition

The best things I did before choosing a program or school to control graduate school expenses were...

I worked for one year before starting graduate school and lived with my parents to save some money, which I spent the following year on tuition and living expenses. It wasn't much but it did reduce the overall amount of what I would eventually take on in loans.

Also, although I went to a more prestigious and therefore expensive graduate school—which I had been advised against--I believe in this economy it is what has made me employable, especially given that my line of work (faith-based organizing) is somewhat non-traditional for my graduate degree (M.Div).

The best things I did during graduate school to control expenses and debt were...

I worked nearly twenty hours a week in positions that complemented my studies. I also had no car, I lived with a roommate in student housing, and instead of going out for drinks or dinner, my friends and I would often cook together multiple times a week, everyone bringing the different ingredients to make whatever meal we had planned at home. But living in New York City, there wasn't a whole lot that I could do to control expenses as much as I would have liked.

What would you do differently?

Instead of working one summer (which was a poorly-paid internship), I wish I had taken more classes to get accreditation in something that I will now have to do in addition to my full-time work (clinical pastoral education, which is required for anyone seeking ordained ministry in the United Church of Christ, which I am). But I do feel that there was little more I could have done to control expenses, and I also believe that the debt I have taken on was a necessary evil to be able to work in a profession in which I feel happy and fulfilled.

Brian P.: Surviving Medical School

Undergraduate Degree: B.A. Psychology – University of Minnesota

Graduate Degree: (in process) M.D. – University of Minnesota

Graduate School: U of M Medical School

Current Position: 3rd Year Medical Student

Note: Thanks to Brian's partner who shared Brian's story from her perspective, as Brian was in the middle of a demanding hospital rotation at the time of this writing.

The best things I did before choosing a program or school to control graduate school expenses were...

Brian applied to 24 different medical schools. His motivation was to get into the best school possible with the most diverse patient population. He was accepted into a number of programs and selected based on prestige of the program.

Medical schools very rarely give any kind of financial help, and although the University of Minnesota did offer Brian a small scholarship, it didn't much influence his decision. He wanted a program that would give him the best education possible, since medical school is a huge financial investment regardless of the institution. Long-term, you get more bang for your buck to attend the best school.

The best things I did during graduate school to control expenses and debt were…

Brian lives with his partner and is able to share expenses with her. They share a car between the two of them, and he often will pack his own coffee and lunch to cut down on day-to-day expenses that can add up quickly. He also manages his budget very closely.

What would you do differently?

Perhaps set savings goals more intentionally with his partner. But in Medical School, again, there is little opportunity either for scholarships, grants, or even part-time work. The best option for cost savings is to get low interest rates and federal loans, which have now been affected by the recent federal debt deal (which will influence Brian's fourth year of medical school loans).

KrisAnne W.: Get Graduate School to Pay You

Undergraduate Degree: Bachelor of Music, Voice Performance; Bachelor of Arts, English — Lawrence University

Graduate Degree: Master of Music, Voice Performance; Doctor of Musical Arts, Voice Performance

Graduate School: University of Minnesota

Current Position: Freelance Musician

The best things I did before choosing a program or school to control graduate school expenses were...

I chose a school that awarded me a huge fellowship and that didn't require me to relocate. My tuition was completely covered for the first year and there was a substantial stipend, with the guarantee of a teaching assistantship for the second year. Along with my performing gigs, it was enough money to live on.

Thanks to the excellent preparation of my undergraduate institution, I was actually offered assistantships outside my major during my subsequent years of study. Between fellowships, assistantships, and scholarships, I was paid to go to school during the entirety of my master's and doctoral studies. I don't think this is possible anymore at the school I attended, so I really did get lucky.

The best things I did during graduate school to control expenses and debt were…

I managed to have tons of fun without spending a lot of money—and yes, making time for your social life is important. My friends and I had great potlucks where everyone contributed and we feasted at home instead of going out. "Breakfast for Dinner" was a favorite theme.

My uncle was getting rid of a beautiful, ridiculous old bar at one point and I put it in my dining room, so we would have drinks at home, or I would host the party and friends would help stock the bar. I also cooked at home from scratch and split groceries with my roommate, which left enough financial wiggle room to grab a cheap lunch or dinner out once a week or so.

What would I do differently?

I honestly wish I would have worked *more* and made payments on my undergraduate loans or funded my IRA while I was in grad school. I was in an unusually good financial situation for a graduate student and I probably could have taken an additional job many semesters without any detrimental effect on my performance. I have always regretted that I didn't study abroad.

Also, I had terrific health insurance as a result of being on the grad assistant plan and I wish I'd used every little benefit it afforded me!

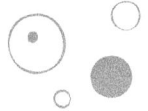

CHAPTER SEVEN

Resources

There are countless resources for information on financial aid. The resources described in this section are examples of helpful, interesting and professional websites, presented here in no particular order.

L ocating financial aid information for graduate school is easy. Identifying which information is trustworthy AND applies to your situation can be a challenge. Start with two or three trustworthy resources that are easy to navigate and understand.

One favorite resource, well worth your time, is the Wiseborrower® Checklist.[33] Created by Access Group, a provider of graduate student loans, this attractive, print-able e-book teaches the twenty-something grad school hopeful how to prepare financially for a successful grad-uate experience. Also, Wayne State University[34] and Loyola University[35] each get an A+ for their web pages on financing options and recent changes to federal loans for graduate and professional students. Both sites are excellent examples of resources available from top-notch financial aid departments.

Each state has a department of higher education that provides information on educational programs in the state as well as financial aid for state residents. Locate your state office and inquire about scholarships, grants or other financial aid for graduate students.

Be cautious about pop-up ads promising scholarship money. If it sounds too good to be true, it probably is. NEVER pay to get a list of scholarships. Finaid.org includes a link to reputable free scholarship databases (http://www.finaid.org/scholarships/other.phtml). Remember, FinAid.org is your first stop (after the

33   http://www.accessgroup.org/campaigns/PreGrad-10/ GettingReadyForSchool/WiseBorrowerCheckList.html
34 http://law.financialaid.wayne.edu/tools.php
35 http://www.loyno.edu/financialaid/ federal-student-loan-changes-2012-2013

campus financial aid office) for reliable, up-to-date information on financial aid.

Web Resources

FinAid (www.Finaid.org)

If you only have time or attention for one financial aid website, make this the one. Begun in 1994 as one guy's public service mission, FinAid.org is nationally recognized as the most reliable independent site for financial aid information.

A few examples of FinAid's topics and resources are:

- *Loans* — Detailed statistics on average student loan debt based on level of education and college type; links to student loan discount information; a Student Loan Checklist to track loans, and help with loan problems —http://www.finaid.org/loans/

- *Scholarships* — Includes links to free, reliable scholarship databases with more than 1.5 million scholarships totaling more than $3.4 billion for students at all educational levels. —http://www.fastweb.com/

- *Student Loan Advisor calculators* for master's and doctoral students:

  - Master's – http://www.finaid.org/calculators/mastersadvisor.phtml

  - Doctoral – http://www.finaid.org/calculators/doctoraladvisor.phtml

In seconds, these calculators identify a maximum manageable student debt load for a given area of study. You'll see the total loan repayment number, an estimated monthly payment, and lots more. One caveat: The estimated starting salaries used in these calculations represent national averages gathered from new grads working full-time in their field of study. This figure does not include those unemployed or working part-time. Plus, allowance should be made to reflect the area of the country where the job is held. Geography (and industry) can have a big impact on starting salary.

Rather than use the pre-assigned salary figure, identify the low end of entry salaries for your field in your area of the country. Within the calculator, mark "other" as your field of study, enter your estimated salary number, then calculate the maximum manageable student debt load. The worst that could happen by guessing low is you hit the jackpot with a plum job and pay off your student loans in two years. See also the Department of Education's Budget Calculator below.

Fastweb (http://www.fastweb.com/)

Fastweb is the free scholarship search site recommended by Finaid.org. Enough said.

Student Aid on the Web (www.studentaid.ed.gov)

This is the official federal student aid site sponsored by the U.S. Department of Education. This agency establishes policies for federal financial aid and is responsible for distributing and monitoring all federal loan funds through approved educational programs. Their website includes detailed information on loans, grants, accreditation and more.

Financial aid information for professional and graduate students is available at: http://studentaid.ed.gov/PORTALSWebApp/students/english/gradstudent.jsp

This *Budget Calculator* helps students quickly estimate financial need during school: http://www2.ed.gov/offices/OSFAP/DirectLoan/BudgetCalc/budget.html

FAFSA (http://www.fafsa.ed.gov/)

The first step to apply for financial aid is to complete a Free Application for Federal Student Aid form. This is the same form you completed for undergraduate financial aid eligibility. A new streamlined version makes this process less cumbersome and painful.

The Student Loan Borrower Assistance Project (http://www.nclc.org/special-projects/student-loan-borrower-assistance.html)

Sponsored by the National Consumer Law Center, this site provides numerous self-help documents, a student loan shopping guide (http://projectonstudentdebt.org/look_leap.vp.html), and direct contact information for ombudsmen at the major student loan and guarantee organizations.

Ask HeatherJarvis (www.Askheatherjarvis.com)

Heather runs a web-based service to help students in high-cost graduate and professional programs navigate the world of student loans before and after graduation. In addition to fee-based individual consultations, Heather offers a ton of free information geared for students in graduate and professional programs. She also provides free webinars on timely topics such as new student loan payback or forgiveness options. If you have a complex student loan question, contact Heather.

The Internal Revenue Service (www.irs.gov/publications)

The free IRS publication, *Tax Benefits for Education*, offers clear and current information about tax benefits related to higher education expenses and student loan interest.

Veterans Administration (www.va.gov)

Information on education benefits available to U.S. military personnel is available at this site.

The National Center for Education Statistics (http://nces.ed.gov/)

This is the primary federal agency that collects and analyzes U.S. educational data. The site contains an excellent college selection tool that includes graduate programs. The tool is titled, "Find the right college for you" and is available at: http://nces.ed.gov/collegenavigator/.

Georgetown University Center on Education and the Workforce (http://cew.georgetown.edu/)

This academic think tank produces free, cutting-edge reports on jobs and education, such as their recent report, *Help Wanted. Projections of Jobs and Education Requirements through 2018.*

Institute for College Access and Success
(http://www.ticas.org/)

This non-profit organization works to make college available and affordable. Their Project on Student Debt offers student loan data and tips to manage loan debt at: http://www.projectonstudentdebt.org.

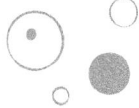

About the Author

Laura H. Gilbert, Ph.D., is the founder of Back to School for Grownups, a higher education practice specializing in the adult learner experience. *Graduate School on a Budget* is the second book in a set on managing college costs. Written in her signature coach-at-your-side style, Dr. Gilbert offers common-sense tips as a professor, coach and three-time graduate student.

Dr. Gilbert's earlier books include *Back to School for Grownups: Your Guide to Making Sound Decisions (November, 2009)* and *How to Save $50,000 on College (May 2011)*, both available in paperback and for Kindle and Nook readers.

As a coach, Dr. Gilbert helps students of all ages identify their educational goals, locate program options, and create a customized plan for academic success. She is a frequent blogger and speaker, is actively involved in policy research, and publishes BTSG News, a monthly e-newsletter. Dr. Gilbert teaches at Concordia University and lives with her family in Minnesota.

Email Dr. Gilbert at laura@saveonyoureducation.com or laura@backtoschoolforgrownups or follow her on Twitter at http://twitter.com/lauragilbertphd